LONELY ROAD

LIFE ON THE BORDERLINE AND INSIDE THE HEAD OF A BORDERLINE PERSONALITY DISORDER, THE DAILY CRAZY LIFE OF A PERSON, LEARNING FROM THE EXPERIENCES OF PEOPLE WHO HAVE WALKED THE SAME ROUTE

LINSY B.

© 2019 Linsy B.

You are welcome to join the Fan's Corner, here

Disclaimer: The experiences detailed in this article are not congruent with any real-life experiences. However, they are reflective of certain people either currently or in the past. This story is meant to be purely anecdotal and to portray the average daily experience of someone struggling with Borderline Personality Disorder.

The information provided here are for information purposes only and do not represent expert views on the subject.

Table of Content

Chapter 1...1

The Story of a BPD Life 1

The Disappointment 3

The Calm 3

The Withdrawal 4

The Relapse 5

No One Truly Understands What You Feel.........7

Why Exactly Do We Do Those Things Even When We Do Not Mean To?...............................9

Chapter 2 17

An Example of a Typical Day for a Woman with BPD...17

Chapter 3...23

Another Typical Day in The Life of a Real BPD Person 23

Timeline of a Struggle...30

Chapter 4...33

Yet Another Typical Day...33

Profile of Victim...33

Another Scenario of a Typical Day 36

Chapter 5...39

Yet Another Typical Day...39

Chapter 6...47

Another Timeline for a Day for a BPD Person ..47

Chapter 7...52

Another Day of a BPD, Somewhat Happy One .52

Chapter 8 58

Exploring Another Typical Daily Timeline for BPD 58

Chapter 9 63

The Signs Have Always Been There 63

BPD Journey Process...65

Chapter 10..70

Life after the Diagnosis.....................................70

Handling Relationships Better 74

Getting Help and Therapy 76

Your Concerns about your Kids........................78

To Sum it Up 81

Each Day is a Constant Struggle 81

Every Emotion is Either Full or Empty.............83

Trust is a Luxury You Cannot Afford 85

Your Default Reaction is to Constantly Assume the Worst 86

You Feel Like You are Just a Passenger in your Body 87

You Desire Validation as If Your Life Depended on It...88

Everything seems Absurd and Crazy 89

You know you are Different................................90

Chapter 1
The Story of a BPD Life

As a person living with borderline personality disorder (BPD), you alone know what pain you feel inside. You struggle in your ability to handle issues as you find that many things are out of your control. Yet despite all your efforts, all you get are a set of eyes judging you, wondering what next act of stupidity they should expect from you.

You see them treading carefully on matters that concern you. Everyone seems very careful not to offend you. You enjoy the attention and the special feeling for a moment only to suddenly have a change in mood where you no longer trust the motive for their action. Are they truly being careful not to hurt your feelings because they love you or because they just think you are trouble? Without knowing it, you assume that they have ulterior motives for their actions. They have something else in mind otherwise they wouldn't be so nice, you say to yourself. Images are conjured up in your head that portrays your feeling as you believe they are in your mind. The images look so real that you struggle within yourself to deny that they are real events, yet they seem real enough. Finally, you cave in, you react to the conjured-up images in your head. Sometimes, it is because you decide to act first and beat them in their game, so you lash out disproportionately in a manner reserved only for the worst offenders who have done massive physical and emotional harm to you.

The Disappointment

Then you notice the shock in their eyes, and you are wondering to yourself, really? Are they claiming not to know what they have done? Such deceitful creatures they are, trying to mask their true intentions with some incredulous make-belief actions. So, you react to the first set of images in your head, lash out and say very hurtful words. You see the hurt in their eyes wondering where all these came from. Then there are new sets of images in your head, even worse than the previous one, so you continue lashing out, vomiting more venom than the previous, the process goes on and on such that even when you try to stop, you are unable to.

The Calm

Finally, you have up to your content's fill. You have finally been able to stop, except that now you feel drained. Look at what you have done, you say to yourself. You try to look apologetically at them. They are still in shock, sometimes they look back with an adulterated form of pity mixed with anger in their eyes. You can't really blame them, can you? As you try to recount what had just happened, you find you hate yourself and the person that you have become.

The Withdrawal

And why shouldn't you hate yourself, you ask without hoping for an answer? What other sensible person will lash out for no reason at the very people they love the most, other than a devil-like yourself, who else could afford to hurt other people the way you do even when they have done nothing to deserve the treatment, you melt out to them?

As you try to cuddle yourself to sleep, you imagine that when you wake up, they may no longer be there. Then another set of images begins showing in your head, clearer than an HD TV screen. Surely, that was their plan all along. They have always wanted to leave anyway and will want to take advantage of this event as an excuse to leave. It is the early phase of your train of thoughts, and you are trying to stop yourself from going that route that your mind keeps racing back and from.

You cannot hold yourself back.

The Relapse

Finally, unable to contain yourself, you lash out again. This time with a different form of accusation. You know they want to leave you alone, which is why they created the situation that will make you lash out and provide a perfect alibi for them to leave and then turn around to claim you are the cause. You go on talking, then your high definition (HD) images switch into the replay of all your loved ones who had abandoned you before, some for far less serious circumstances as this. You feel this dread inside of you. You do not want to lose them. Please don't go, you wish to say to them. Yet, it is not those words that come out of your mouth. Instead, it is the very words that will make any sensible person walk out the door and never look back that comes out from your mouth. A part of you knows you are doing things the wrong way, yet you find you are unable to stop yourself. You look for signs, any sign at all of them to hang on to that they will not leave. Even when they try to reassure you, their words sound like people who are only trying to pacify you before making their next move. Every suspicious move of theirs is interpreted to mean they intend to carry on with their plan to leave you alone and abandon you.

Then you become desperate. You decide to take drastic actions and blackmail them into staying. What better way to do that than to claim you were going to hurt yourself? Your threat seems to have some effect or does it? Then to show you are not joking, you inflict some harm on your body.

No One Truly Understands What You Feel

That is a typical story, and you wonder how a day that had started like any normal day has descended rapidly into a day where you are probably at the hospital where they now seem to know you because of your frequent visit from self-inflicted injuries. You cry yourself out, swearing never again to go this route again. Surely, you will be able to stop yourself before any of these happens, right? Apparently not.

For people who do not have BPD, all they see in you is a dysfunctional person, who by the way they have analyzed, researched and written documents upon documents on. But do they understand it from the point of view of a BPD? Do they know what it is like to be living with BPD? As a matter of fact, you only need to have five out of these nine symptoms to be classified as BPD, which means, you only need to get 56% and you would have crossed the pass mark for being qualified to be called a BPD. Anyway, these symptoms are what they see from people who have BPD;

- Intense fear of feelings of rejection or abandonment, even to the point of using extreme means to avoid these perceived separation, abandonment or rejection whether they are real or imagined

- A series of intense unstable relationships that alternate between idealizing a person, one moment and then devaluing them the next minute and imagining them to be persons who are not caring enough

- Experience frequent changes in self-image and identity that is characterized by frequent changes in self-goals and values, and believing yourself to be bad or not existing at all

- Live with moments stress-induced paranoia and lose touch with reality, which can last from a few minutes to a few hours

- Threaten suicide, self-injury, especially when used as a way of responding to fears of abandonment or rejection.

- Display a wide range of swings in mood that can last for a couple of hours to a few days and characterize by intense joy, irritation, shame or anxiety

- Regular feelings of being empty

Why Exactly Do We Do Those Things Even When We Do Not Mean To?

What many people do not know about BPD is that struggling with borderline personality disorder can be likened or compared to a continuous war inside one's head like a big roller coaster that never ends. The challenge is not only real but almost like a challenge that is a full blast all the time leaving you to fight on one side or the other and sometimes you are just helpless as the war in your head ranges on.

As a BPD, you have to struggle with three major forms of emotions; shame, guilt, and anger as they take turn to control how you act and react to issues. They influence all your impulsive and non-impulsive actions.

Only a person with BPD can understand how extremely difficult it is to keep up with these conflicting emotions and thoughts. Despite your best efforts to change, yet every day you wake up, you are never sure of what kinds of triggers to expect during the day. You are never sure if it will be what you see, things you hear or just some imaginary thoughts within your head, the results are basically the same with your emotions flying everywhere at a rate that is so hard to keep up with, fast and spinning your head to the extent you no longer have any idea what happens around you and the effects of those actions on those who are unfortunate to be at the vicinity of where you are or are victims of your outburst.

The life of a BPD is a lonely one because by now you would have unintentionally pushed all those who would have loved you away, so that you feel isolated and rejected, which is probably one of the worst feeling a BPD can have. You know your actions are pushing them away, but you are only really trying to keep them, which is why you do the things you do in the ways you know how to do it, but then, it seems what you do is never enough, you are never right, you are empty and do not know how to do the right things. But then you wonder, if they know this much about you, why do they still leave. Your logical brain understands, but our emotions refuse to accept the reasons as being enough.

Then there are those moments when being alone, curled up is all that you wish for, you want to hide away from yourself, everyone, and most importantly your emotions. The problem is, you are never sure what side of you is coming next and why.

One common thing with BPDs is the trauma of waking up each morning, every BPD you know say that waking up is a constant struggle morning after mornings. When you finally overcome the inertia of waking up, you have to go through the harrowing experience of having to prepare for the activities of the day. You try to plan for what to expect during the day and make a mental note of ensuring that nothing is left behind, that you do not forget anything which brings with it another form of stress. This stress is compounded with the fact that you are never sure of what you are going to do during the day, even if you have a carefully planned calendar and a schedule of things to do, you are never sure if you are going to cancel any of those plans at the last minute. When you finally muster up the energy to get up in the morning, nothing can describe the pathetic emotion you feel inside. You beat yourself up even before the day starts, you beat yourself up for being who you are, for not being able to get anything right. Then you beat yourself for beating yourself up despite promising yourself not to do it again and then the vicious cycle goes on and on with an unstoppable force that you are never going to win.

As part of the process of getting ready after managing to get up from the bed, you prepare mentally for having to leave the safety nest of your home and end up spending hours getting dressed, packing your bag with your medication and sensory items that sometimes help in grounding you during anxious situations.

As soon as you get out of the house, you immediately begin looking like a fish out of water, completely overwhelmed being amidst people. Seeing that other people can get on easily with their life and function normally when you have all these racing thoughts and feelings fighting for a place in your head does not make it any easier. Even the slightest noise, an innocent push by somebody, or just imagining a person is looking at you in a certain kind of way can be a trigger for the thoughts and anxiety flooding your head and then all you want to do next is just run, run as far away as possible and as quickly as you can.

For a BPD, leaving the house is probably considered as one of the successful days, on days when the chaos and struggle is at its peak, it becomes difficult to leave the house, it does not matter if you are supposed to be in school, at work or have a date or meeting scheduled, you simply do not leave the house. You are scared of what might happen, your heart racing all the while. On such days, you feel your world closing in as if you are not going to make it to the next minute like you would just pass out and die just there and then. Yet, you wish that this passes quickly as you have been told it would, but the worst of these is knowing that those around you not knowing the tremor going on inside your head, except the emphatic ones who understand what you are going through.

The life of a BPD feels and looks like every bit of a test where you are having to face numerous hazards along the way throughout the day. Some of those hazards will successfully hit and throw you to the ground, others will just lurk around waiting for any available opportunity to be unleashed to test your ability to cope with the intense emotional trauma you are going to feel. Through those moments of emotional chaos, whether it is the issue of missing a day or facing a breakup, your brain interprets it the same way and produces the same reaction, which always frightens other people who do not understand what is happening.

For a BPD, everything suffers, be it work, school, business, social meetings, everything suffers, even the things that could have been helpful. Why wouldn't they suffer when you are constantly bombarded with mood swings, interrupted only anxiety, rage, self-harm, and suicidal thoughts. Your difficulty in regulating your emotions will always mean you are unable to control your impulses and experience chronic feelings of emptiness.

One of the most challenging facts of being a BPD is the frustrating cyclic process of the experience by reducing the person to a completely irrational human being even if they are in a profession that is logical and evidence-based. You will struggle to give people the benefit of the doubt even when the said persons have not yet given you a reason to doubt them and make wide accusations and conclusions that have no bearing to any reality on the ground.

Chapter 2

An Example of a Typical Day for a Woman with BPD

A typical day for a BPD, although time may vary.

Profile of Victim

Meet 24-year-old Jane, a computer analyst and in a relationship. She represents our first use case.

The alarm goes off at 6 am, you snooze it for a while.

You finally get out of bed and start getting ready. Arrive at work at 7:50 am.

You send a good morning text to your boyfriend, as you wait for your computer to boot in what you hope will be a very productive day of work.

It's been about a minute and he still hasn't responded as you check your phone for the umpteenth time. You try to console yourself that it's okay, maybe he's still doing his business on the loo or something else is taking his time. So, you decide to ignore him for a while and settle down to the day's work, you start by opening your emails and read the ones that seem useful, delete the ones that look like junk. You continue like that for a bit while keeping an eye on the phone. Damn, it has been the whole of 10 minutes, and he still hasn't responded, you wonder if there is a problem, especially since it took him just 3 mins to respond the last time. Then your mind goes into a race wondering what he could possibly be doing. Perhaps he now despises you for being so clingy and needy, then you become anxious and wonder if you have done the right thing texting him good morning.

You begin to get paranoia as you try to convince yourself there is nothing to worry about, after all, he has so far proven to be trustworthy, that should be reassuring, shouldn't it? As you try to internalize that.

You try buying time by engaging in other activities to distract yourself by engaging in work. Okay, the truth is, you are not distracted enough as you check your phone repeatedly trying to put the rapidly developing anxiety under control. Now, with no response still forthcoming, you begin to panic and imagine that he must obviously hate you and is probably on a dating site and meeting someone new who is probably not as needy as you are, someone with more beautiful and sexier outlook, someone better than you in many ways.

After a long time, he texts back, then you experience a drastic change in mood, then you begin to feel he doesn't hate you, after all, you do love him so much and are so happy. Then another voice whispers to you, and you are wondering why he didn't make an effort to keep up the conversation almost as if he is not interested in you again, maybe it is because you are not that attractive, maybe you need to slim down a little and do some touch-ups. Then you begin going through a mental list of the things you believe to be wrong with you. You subsequently decide to make yourself thinner, so that he can get to like you again. You then decide to start immediately by skipping lunch for that day.

All this while, work gets to suffer as nothing productive gets done since a substantial part of the time is spent peeping at your phone every second and anxious thought flick through your mind about your boyfriend. Then you realize it is almost close of business for the day, and he still hasn't reached out to you after replying to the good morning text and that was more than 6 hours ago. By now, your mind is on hyperdrive wondering if it is a good idea to send him another message. You then type a text message and consider deleting it so that he does not consider you needy, then you scrutinize it again before you finally send him a text. A message enters your phone soon after, and you rush to pick up the phone and see that the message is not from him. You are disappointed.

You are close to your house and there is still no message from him, you are in full panic mode by now and have texted him with another needy, disgusting and insulting message, even then he still does not respond.

After an extended period of complete panic mode and where you are horrified, you start to convince yourself that he is never going to call you ever again, you are fat, ugly and not attractive to him, so you make up your mind to win him back at all cost from whoever may be trying to snatch him away from you. You see your life as a complete wretch without him, with no life, no friends, no passion, no hobbies, and your life is dependent on him. By now you are convinced you are worthless and not useful, so you make up your mind to apologize and start typing an apology text when his message comes in saying he had a fruitful and busy day.

Wow, that was close, suddenly he looks so great, such a remarkable and gentle guy that you imagine a blissful life with him. You can imagine how much love you guys will have together. You respond promptly to his text message, yet 10 mins later, there is no response from him and so the whole cycle continues.

Chapter 3

Another Typical Day in The Life of a Real BPD Person

Profile of Victim

Meet Mary, 19 years old, not yet sure what to be in life.

You struggle to shake yourself out from sleep every morning because you dread having to wake up and would much prefer both your good and the bad dream world of intense adventure after adventure. On your bad day, you would rather stay in bed and continue to live in your dreamland that removes your true reality.

You constantly probe for some form of motivation for waking up and getting out of bed even though you know you have important things to do that involves other people, it is not those things that get you to wake up, it could sometimes be the thought of having coffee that provides you the required motivation to get out of bed as you struggle to focus on reality.

And then it all starts coming back. You are pondering why you are stuck in life, why the heck you are still alone, how come you are getting so old so quickly?

You then consciously decide to focus and attempt to plan for the day's activities which results in a fury of ideas as you try to concentrate on just a few of them so you do not end up diverting your mind. Any activity for the day that requires that you act normally or maturely freak you out because you try to imagine the amount of shame you feel and how worthless you are as a person.

The loneliness you experience is overwhelming, and you wish you had someone who could understand you and not judge you for whom you are, you reach out to a few persons who you believe may be able to slow down the definite path you know your mind is racing to, yet at the end of the call, you do not seem to feel any better.

Social media is a no-go area for you because it makes you feel depressed and sulky especially Facebook and Instagram. Unlike the others which are a total nightmare to you, twitter is a little better because it allows you to connect with other

BPDs or mental health fighters in the same shoes as you are. You avoid as much as possible looking at the timeline of anyone.

By this time your thoughts are racing everywhere as you struggle desperately to focus on doing one thing at a time. It is not long after that you feel weary as you search for anything to generate a spark in you so that you do not panic and get overwhelmed. You try watching a movie, read some magazines or journals, or scribble down your thoughts in a notepad, none of which seem to have the desired effect.

Next comes the headache, the freaking out and then anger, which leads you to lash out at those around you. It is worse if you have an event scheduled for the day and have to meet some people or an invitation you have to honor even if you have been preparing for it for some time, you make up an excuse not to attend or simply turn off your phone so you do not get any call from anyone to convince you otherwise. You even turn off your phone on your birthday. A part of you wish to hear the birthday wishes, but there is the other part of you that is not sure how best to respond to a flurry of messages on your birthday. When possible, you try to disassociate yourself by trying to get some more sleep or drink some wine or take some medication.

It is worse if you are pre menstruating, you get depressed, nauseating and even suicidal. Sometimes, for many months on end, you find you are unable to function well enough to keep up a job and even find it difficult to apply for jobs or respond to applications. It can be crazy.

You can go into unprovoked arguments, screaming, shouting, and breaking down, then, there is the unexplained guilt over what you perceive to be a day of offending the people around you and sometimes, they were not even offended in the first place, it was just a normal banter.

Sometimes to ease off, you go on long walks or jog pretending to be on serious walkout so that you do not have to say hello to anyone. You avoid going out or attending to your stuff until they get urgent, then you are desperate and develop another period of anxiety.

On the days you do manage to go out, you avoid the gaze of others and wear a headphone because you are conscious of the people around you as you imagine they may be staring at you. You are uncomfortable, this was why you never wanted to go out in the first place. You imagine everyone to be against you, so you are rude to everyone, taxi drivers, doctors, waiters, sellers, no one is spared of your rash and insolent comments.

At the end of it all, you suffer a nervous breakdown and wish you could turn back the hands of time and not act so rashly to all those people who you recognize didn't deserve what they endured in your hands. Sometimes, it is for no apparent reason, and you find that you lose all sense of reality and wish there was a way to relieve the emotional pain you feel, the pain can be so bad that you try to replace it with a physical pain and so you end up cutting yourself or even pulling your hair out.

There are days when you are unsure if you are just having a bad memory, or if it is a dream or something that happened. Life can seem meaningless and strange, shameful thoughts fill up your mind as time seems to stand still. Subsequently, you pass out, sometimes you wake up in the same place where you passed out, sometimes, you are surrounded by a sea of concerned faces, other times you wake up in a hospital or some health or mental health facility.

On a good day, you are in unusually high sprit, chanting, singing and playful. You even go into a prolonged conversation with your family members and even strangers. You show enough concern as you find out about their feelings and things that concern them.

Timeline of a Struggle

Profile of Victim

Meet Melaine, 30 years old, a mother in New York

6 am: You open your eyes for the first time like someone who got punched in the face.

7:30 am: After overcoming the struggle to wake up despite knowing the baby is hungry and requires some attention, you force yourself to get up for the day. The more senior boy has already turned the house into a mess while the baby by now is crying to have his diapers changed.

8:20 am: You change the baby's diaper and check up on the older boy as you prepare for the cleaning up you plan to do that day. The boy by now is having his cereals, throwing tantrums and turning the whole house upside down, stirring up an emotion inside you that makes you feel like a failed parent as you struggle to hold back your tears wondering if the kids were not better off without you. The next minute he does something really admirable, and you feel so happy and tell yourself you cannot let them out of your sight for any reason.

11:00 am: You go through your activities of the day and experience up and down emotions. Some days, you are fortunate to be unusually happy throughout the day, other days you are not that lucky, and you get paranoia. On bad days, you find yourself questioning your very existence, wondering if you are not just filling up an undeserved space in the world, fortunately, you imagine your kids without a mother which helps to restrain you from considering suicide. You decide to employ that as a motivation to want to keep going and stay alive.

1:30: As the day progresses, your mind goes on hyperdrive. You start imagining irrational things happening, like news coming from your husband's workplace of him dying, or the baby having convulsion and dying in the process or the older boy getting lost in the woods or stolen by some kidnapper.

6:30 pm: Husband is supposed to be home by now, he was home 6:24 pm the day before, or did he, in fact, die as you had imagined he would? If he dies, does he have a will in place? What will you tell the kids? Then you imagine you always knew he would die young which was why you never wanted to marry him in the first place. You detest him for dying so soon and abandoning the responsibilities of the kids to you. Not long after, you hear him come into the driveway with his familiar hunk. He is alive after all, and you love him and intend to spend the rest of your life with him.

11:40 pm: You try and get yourself to sleep and expect a troubled night.

Chapter 4
Yet Another Typical Day

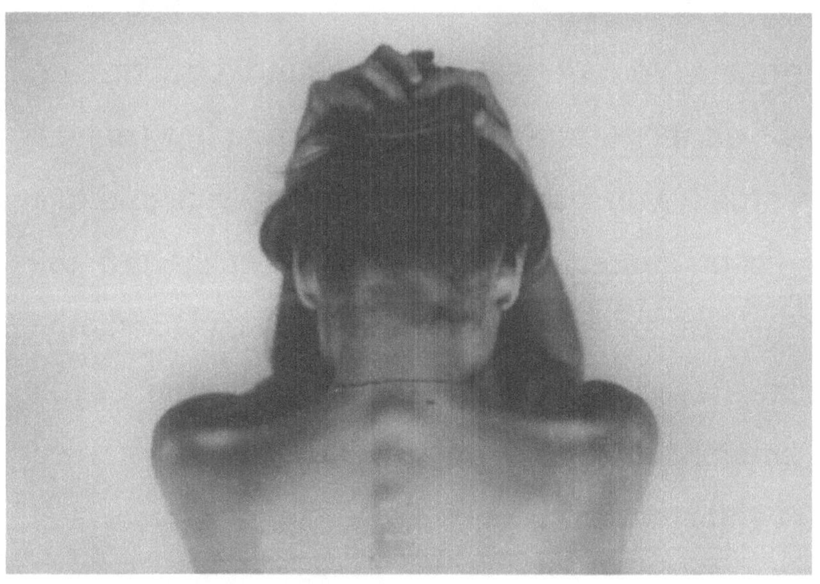

Profile of Victim

Let's meet Diane, 26 years old, a sales rep. at a real estate agency and in a relationship.

7:00 am: Typically, you struggle to wake up and when you do, you feel cranky, depressed and miserable knowing you will have to face another day. You discover boyfriend is no longer by your side on the bed, you go into a panic, then you hear a sound in the kitchen as he calls you to know if you are awake.

8:00 am: You are still idling around, checking up news on the internet, saying hello to a few friends, eventually you glance at the time and you go into a panic of going late to work. You rush into the bathroom for a shower while you try to soothe your nerves and reduce the anxiety attack. You ultimately make it through with getting dressed and going to work.

9:05 am: You get to the office slightly late, immediately you begin to feel guilty and ashamed, almost go into a panic mode. You consciously try to create an image of a professional outlook and say hi to a few colleagues even though your mind is racing all over the place. You finally make it to your workstation in one piece, as you turn on your computer even though more than anything you wish you were not at work that day or any day for that matter.

9:50 am: You are irritated at everything happening to you and sliding gradually into a panic mode. Your computer screen seems to be too bright, the USB cable is not long enough, the internet is slow, the programs hanging and even the mouse seem not to be moving. The whole room seems to be too dark and hot. Eventually, you manage to make it up to lunchtime.

1:30 pm: You return from your lunch break feeling a lot better. You seem more alive, alert and ready to work.

4:30-5pm: You stare at your watch and notice you have made significant progress with your work. You feel that great sense of accomplishment and are even raring to go on working.

6-7pm: By now you are apparently terribly tired, but it happens to be one of the days when you don't seem to want to stop working, eventually you have no choice but to go home.

7:30 pm: You get your things ready as you prepare to go home.

8 pm: You arrive at home, suddenly you feel like a piece of shit, exhausted, cranky and miserable, but the warm welcome from your boyfriend helps to make you feel slightly better.

9 pm: You go through the rest of the evening catching up with the day's activity until you eventually go to bed.

Another Scenario of a Typical Day

Profile of Victim

Let's meet Sue, a mother, 34 years old and customer fulfilment's agent at a retail outlet.

For you, maybe every day is emotionally draining both physically and mentally. Perhaps your job is a very physical one that requires a lot of work that leaves you in physical exhaustion and pain. Despite being tired, you are unable to sleep properly and always having interrupted night of sleep. You have sex with your husband in-between, but the rest of the night is used for tossing and turning on the bed before eventually truly dozing off. Consequently, you tend to always wake up with a headache and feel sore as you slowly make your way out of the bed and grab a cup of coffee before going to shower.

You and hubby drop the kids at school as you both make your way to work.

You are fortunate, contented and live a happy life, but your facial expressions always seem to tell a different story. It does not matter if you are delighted, glum, laughing, angry or being emotional, your facial expression is the same boring, bitchy, and void appearance, except when you are under the influence of alcohol. Despite trying to practice in front of a mirror, you have not achieved any success. You are lucky, though; your husband does not fall into the category of those who cannot interpret your facial expression.

For weekends, your routine is a little different. On Saturdays, you do not have to wake up early, when you do, you get to do some cleaning up, go for grocery shopping, go to the cinema or hang out at the local bar.

Chapter 5
Yet Another Typical Day

Profile of Victim

Meet James, in a relationship, 32 years old and computer analyst.

6:00 am: The alarm from your phone rouses you up as it begins to ring as you perceive the sound in your head. Your body still feels like someone who had received a pounding the day before. You barely slept for three and a half hours. You make a mental note to go to bed early, but you have made and broken that same commitment every day. Despite your exhaustion, you take your dose of pills with a glass of water, hoping it accomplishes its work of making you have more control over your emotions.

6:30 am: You still feel tired even though you have been awake for about 30 mins and not able to leave the confines of your bed, for unexplained reasons, you sometimes feel more exhausted when trying to wake up than you do when trying to sleep. Not wanting to go to work late, you finally force yourself out of bed, even though your brain wants you to stay longer in bed.

7:30 am: You prepare a quick breakfast and set the coffee machine rolling and do the dishes while listening to the morning news. You ultimately make it to the shower, apply the cream on your body, wear your clothes, put on your shoes and put finishing touches to your outfit.

9:00 am: You are already at work, but the early morning tiredness has refused to ease off. You are wondering if the others have noticed how tired you are already, and they already believe you are lazy and don't add any value to the company. Or maybe, they do not care about you. Then you start worrying about your job and for how long management will continue to tolerate you. Who knows, they may even be preparing your sack letter right now. You start considering a backup plan in your head, you open some job sites for suitable openings, and you end up not focusing on the actual task you have to do.

10:30 am: After a long time, you begin to calm down since it seems like everyone else is engrossed in their work and no one seems to be making a move to sack you. Then it hits you. Your girlfriend hasn't texted or called you since morning. You are wondering if she loves you, even though you have heard her say it every day. You mentally spank yourself, you are overthinking things again as you try to restrain yourself and fight back your fears of abandonment.

11:00 am: You realized you were famished and pondering why no one has cared to inquire from you if you have eaten. You are wandering towards anorexia, even though it is not deliberate. Fortunately, you have been productive at work and have made some progress.

1:00 pm: So far you have made it to lunchtime without any notable incident. You take the second round of your daily recommended pills, after which you have lunch.

2:30 pm: As the day goes by, you are assigned more easy responsibilities, but you find you are having difficulty concentrating on the task even though you know it needs to get done and so frustration is setting it. The frustration further makes it more difficult to concentrate.

3:30 pm: Despite the frustration, you successfully complete the work and even make suggestions to your boss on what you believe will improve how things can be done at work. You feel offended because it seems your boss didn't promptly accept and implement the idea. You know there is no need to feel offended because your boss was very clear that the present system works just fine and even appreciated the suggestion, even then you can feel your emotion splitting and suddenly the world becomes good and bad with anger and frustration now the only thing you now feel towards your workplace. The desire to quit is rekindled and once again you lose focus. You visit the job site you left earlier in the morning.

4:00 pm: Ultimately, common sense prevails as you remind yourself that your job is a cool one with some of the most remarkable set of people who support and appreciate you and your endeavors. You then wonder what you were thinking and feel guilty and stupid for thinking that way losing an hour of focus over nothing. You now try to make up for the lost time by working extra hard when you eventually calm down.

5:00 pm: Finally, it is close of business and It's time to go home, even though you do not feel excited about it because of the unattended chores that have to be attended to. You know you cannot postpone the chores again as your girlfriend is expected to visit later in the day and you do not want her complaining about your apartment.

7:00 pm: You are finally able to complete all the tasks you have been deferring, everywhere looks okay right now. You decide to check your phone only to see a text from your girlfriend saying she has a lot of workloads at school and cannot drop by tonight. Even though logically you understand, your emotions nonetheless take the better of you as you begin to lose control. The splitting spirit comes upon you again as you classify both good and bad. You consider discontinuing the relationship and moving on as you believe this is just an excuse to abandon you. Maybe you should download a dating app and find someone else as you feel unloved, sad, abandoned and angry. You decide to take dinner alone, after which you calm down sufficiently to feel better.

8:00 pm: Next you find yourself taking stock of your life and find that you do not have friends around as that familiar feeling of abandonment starts to creep into your mind. You seem not to get any kind of understanding from anyone. It takes a great amount of effort as you attempt to bring your emotions under control and try to distract yourself by watching your favorite show on TV.

9:00 pm: Contrary to your expectation, the TV show has not had the desired effect, instead, your emotion has completely gone out control, you feel like you are drowning as if you have been struck by a volcanic eruption. This feeling is so great as you begin to search for what can be a solution for you and pull a bottle of Maltin from the cabinet even though you know it doesn't help yet your emotion doesn't subside.

11:00 pm: You struggle now to maintain a quiet mind and try to meditate as recommended by the therapist, but you are finding it hard to do so and so you get frustrated and give it up. Perhaps you decide it is time to go to bed, and with no sleep, you opt instead to now read a book.

1:00 am: By now the frustration is getting out of hand as you still cannot get to sleep. You expend a significant part of your time staring at the ceiling, tossing from one side of the bed to the other. Various thoughts of your failure flood your mind of various task you planned to accomplish but couldn't with no thoughts spared for the ones you were able to successfully do.

3:00 am: At last, you are able to fall asleep after more than 5 hours you had planned to go to bed. Tomorrow (actually) today is another day.

Chapter 6
Another Timeline for a Day for a BPD Person

Profile of Victim

Let us meet 20-year-old Jilly from Florida. She is a student and single.

Your day seems to be a series of mood swing that undergoes periods of crests and troughs. At times you are full of energy like a hyperactive child, yet the very next day you could be all moody and want to have nothing to do with anyone. You also notice there are moments when fellow students are comfortable having small talks with you and other moments when they beat a retreat as soon as they detect the look in your eyes.

So, on certain days you sleep until it is noon.

1 or 2 pm: You know you are supposed to be in school, yet you can't get yourself to stand up from the bed, you are wondering if you want to go.

3 pm: You do get out of bed, but it is not to go to school, instead you measure how much weight you

have gained or lost and make some tea for yourself.

4 pm: You look at your room and imagine it can look a lot neater than it presently is, but you postpone the cleaning for another day as you have done in the last few days.

6 pm: You are back in bed and have a bad dream of your boyfriend breaking up with you. You decide to get up and do something useful.

6:30 pm: You decide to take a bath in an attempt to reduce the misery you are experiencing as a result of the cold. You feel an urge to injure yourself while in the bath and hoping that the water will wash off the blood easily and you will be fine. You ultimately overcome the urge, get through with your bath and avoid eating dinner.

9:00 pm: You recognize the urge to cut yourself was your emotions going haywire and have the presence of mind to take your medication. You check your weight again and switch on your laptop and look for at YouTube for anything interesting enough to distract you and fight the suicidal thoughts that are beginning to creep in.

10 pm: You decide to be naughty and place a phone sex ad on Craigslist while you wait for sex-starved, strange men who desire phone sex to call you hoping that will make you feel better.

11:00 pm: You ultimately decide you have had enough for the day and go to eat dinner. You subsequently decide to watch a movie before going to sleep.

12:30 am: You decide to go back to bed and find out what is happening in the social media space. You check out Instagram and you are wondering why the lives of other people seem to be so good while yours seems to be a chaotic one. You begin getting into panic mode, yet you do not drop the phone.

1:30 am: You finally summon the strength to drop the phone and devote the next two hours in trying to fall asleep instead you find you are restless and anxious. You wonder to yourself if today is not the best day to end it all, you decide to hang on a little and wait to be sure everyone is asleep before you do it. Your body then begins yearning for a cigarette, weed or any other coping mechanism even though you know from experience that they are unhealthy. Eventually, you have what looks like a semblance of sleep, but you'll also wake up periodically throughout the night.

Chapter 7
Another Day of a BPD, Somewhat Happy One

Profile of Victim

Jay is 28 years old, she is an attorney and works at one of the leading law firms in the country. She is engaged.

You wake up even though the alarm is not due to ring until about 30 minutes from now. This has become a regular incidence now as your brain rarely allows you to enjoy a full night of sleep. You cannot help it as you wake up groggy which contributes to making your anxiety start every morning. You recognize that when you do not sleep soundly, you tend to lose "Frogger."

You decide to make good use of rising early and make a mental plan of the day's schedule. You are scheduled to return home today after a few days of vacation with your fiancé. You run through the various possible scenario, the possibility of something bad happening along the way on your journey back or you are forgetting your items on the shelf of the bathtub and anything your mind can conjure up.

Ultimately, you turn towards your partner as your heart fills with joy and you feel the love you have for him is nothing like you have felt before. The feeling is so strong you seem to be floating on cloud nine. But as he continues to sleep and snore, you ponder what you cherish about him and why he is so selfish to still be sleeping even when you are unable to sleep. You start loathing him gradually as you convince yourself he deliberately tries to rest properly each day to your detriment. You wish he also suffers as you suffer and doubt if he loves you as he claims.

Eventually, he wakes up and puts on a smile as he sees you are awake. He proceeds to kiss you on your forehead, and you find you are back in love again with the bad feelings disappearing as quickly as it had come.

You ultimately decide to head to the bathroom and stand in front of the mirror naked and start to observe everything you hate about yourself. You imagine acne on your face, the fats in your stomach and small boobs until you can successfully pull yourself away from the mirror to continue with getting ready.

After a while, you eventually find something that convinces you to be a superstar and your face lights up. You complete your bath and get into your clothes and come out with a spring in your steps.

At the airport, you imagine everyone is admiring you as the superstar that you are, you have a nice smile for everyone. On the plane, you are all over your partner as you discuss nothing, in particular, just having a good time with him. At some point, you get into a debate, then an argument and then it gets heated and you lash out in anger He looks away and keeps up the conversation with a straight face. Your feelings for him begin making a U-turn, you draw up a mental list of his faults and how it is his fault that you are feeling moody. You realize he is aware as he picks up a book to read while you follow suit.

Eventually, you drop your book and sink into your seat as you prepare to spend the remaining time of the flight wallowing in self-pity. You discover you are no longer the superstar you were before you entered the plane. You notice you hate everyone around you, the other passengers, the flight attendants and most importantly, you hate yourself.

Amidst all that, you finally fall asleep and feel a lot better by the time you wake up. Your anxiety has subsided, and you disembark from the plane. Your fiancé looks amazing once again as you guys hold hands towards the taxi.

At home, you are still in a good mood as you try cleaning up your space and putting clutters in place. Your emotions are like you are floating about the ground and extremely happy. Your Frogger has crossed the road and all your troubles are far from you at the moment and you relish the happiness you feel even though you do not know how long it will last.

At long last, you lie on your bed as you try to sleep and drift into the dream world.

Chapter 8
Exploring Another Typical Daily Timeline for BPD

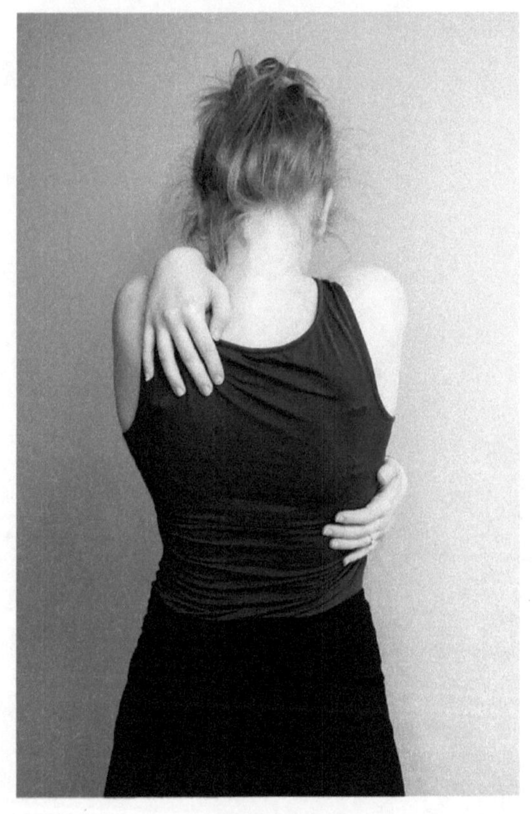

Profile of Victim

Meet 32-year-old Mari, runs her business and single

9:00 am.: You are awake but are asking yourself if slept at all last night or even awake yet. Even though you do not want to go to Facebook you still check it out and leave there wondering Why everyone seems to employ it as a platform to flaunt their fortunate lives in your face. You subsequently tell yourself that moving from the bed hurts and contemplate staying still. You remember you had a dream at night that you are trying to figure out the meaning. You wonder what the day will bring.

10:00 am.: You finally crawl out of bed after convincing yourself that you are awake, and it is time for breakfast and should probably get dressed. The urge for a cigarette is strong, so you cave in, yet you do not feel any better. You consider the task of brushing your teeth hard, you finally get around to doing it, and feel better about yourself.

10:45 am.: Now you are all dressed up and feel too tired to wear makeup. It is a lot of work. You are unsure if you should go out or not and what good going out will do for you.

11:00 am.: You spend the next one hour trying to convince yourself to wear makeup and how it can make you feel good and induce you to go out. You are then distracted by a video and funny meme, which leaves you pondering why your own life is different from that of others, why you live a lonely life.

Noon: You finally decide to take a nap as you see everything around you as hurting. Unable to take that nap you decide to do some chores instead.

1:00 pm.: You seem to be able to get some shit done. Notwithstanding, there is still a lot to achieve, at least there is some progress. It seems to have had a positive effect on you as you feel a lot better than you were formerly.

1:15 pm.: You instantly see yourself as a strong, independent woman who does not need a man in her life. You promise yourself to turn your life around and be a superstar and shame those who do not believe in you. You decide you are going to be single for the rest of your life.

1:20 pm.: You begin to feel sad and go into a panic attack thinking only of how to injure yourself believing it will make you snap out of the panic attack. With each passing minute, you seem to be sucked in.

1:30 pm. Now you are in serious panic mode and wonder if you should contact someone, but then there is no one left who still understands you or is patient enough to still take your shit. You remember there is a cat in the house. He can provide some succor you believe.

2:00 pm: You yearn for some human company as you take your lunch.

3:00 pm.: You find you are sleepy and sleep on the couch.

5:30 pm.: You are back awake and feel refreshed.

6:00 pm.: Looks like someone is home as you perceive sounds from the TV.

6:30 pm.: Your mood begins returning as you begin getting angry at the cat, the person around and even the TV for being so loud.

7:50 pm.: You are no longer in the mood to play with the cat as he has become a nuisance. All you want to do is to punch someone in the face.

9:00 pm.: By now you have enjoyed your bath, had dinner and settled down to watch a talk show on TV. Everything seems very fine, you are in an upbeat mood, the cat is cuddling you, the program on TV is interesting so far.

11:30 pm.: You feel exhausted. It is time for your next round of medication.

12:35 pm.: You lie on your bed as you try to sleep.

Chapter 9
The Signs Have Always Been There

For many people, they are unable to tell they have BPD until their early adulthood. As a teenager with BPD, it is hard to tell if your strong reactions to issues are as a result of just being a shitty teenager or if your feelings justify why you act the way you do. A greater part of your time will be attempting to figure out why everyone else is at fault for every incident. But somehow, you always know there was something about how different from the others your reaction was to issues.

In addition to the normal self-image struggle as a teenager, a BPD will feel an extra feeling of no one interested in being friends with you, and because you assume no one wants to be friends with you, you begin to act shitty to friends. After a while, you sort of rationalize it as a way for you to stay sane. Yet deep down you feel there is something wrong that has to stop, only that you feel helpless in stopping it. Unlike other teenagers, you begin to develop a history of cutting and harming yourself in various ways and go for therapy more often than the others do as you struggle with emotional regulation.

They were the frequent moment of highs, really highs, lows and really lows with some of these changes happening within minutes of each other. Some of these feelings happen so quickly that you are unable to keep track of why and how you feel the way you do. There will be moments when you consider being hit by a bus was not such a bad ideal, you imagine that the world would move on and be a better place without you in it.

BPD Journey Process

Dealing with Anger

When it comes to the issue of anger management, it is almost always a short trigger. The anger will be hot, quick, and then it would burn out almost as quickly followed by an almost equal intensity of guilt and shame. Everyone is viewed with suspicion so that you end up cutting off relationships with loved ones and others around you. Because of that, you try to second guess them and break up with them before they get the chance to break up with you and make others feel a part of the pain that you continuously live with.

Even then, this part of you yearns to interact with people and enjoy a normal and functional relationship with others, but you also feel it is not going to happen. Who could possibly know the kind of person you are and want to stay with you either as a friend or in a relationship, who would want to put up with the kind of stuff you exhibit? There are moments when you believe the situation will be something you can easily manage yet when it comes upon you, you see yourself as out of control.

Handling Relationships

One critical component of BPD is that things are either very dark or they are very white, to find gray areas, you have to work really hard. Consequently, when you are in a relationship, passions can get intense at times and you place your partner on a high pedestal, in such moments when it is good, it feels tremendously great. You see your partner as being lovely and very supportive that you cannot imagine life without them.

However, on the other side of the coin, you are never trusting your partner, believing it is only a matter of time you are going to be cheated on, so you are flipping in and out of paranoia, and on some of such flips, you would believe you hate the person. After a while, you will discover you have sabotaged many great relationships because your partner is unable to decipher whether the moments in which you adore them are stronger than those moments where you hate them. In the end, the whole drama ruins the relationship and leaves you completely broken, ashamed, guilty and sometimes completely blindsided in your expectation of the breakup.

Then you start replaying all the shitty things you targeted at your partner now ex, the borderline emotional abuse and all the manipulative stunts you pulled on them believing at that time, you were doing it for your emotional stability.

Finally, You Have the Diagnosis

Sometimes it takes a while to finally figure out who you really are. As you pay more frequent visits to the doctors, then the possibility of you being a borderline begins to show up, more often than not, they will misdiagnose you for bipolar because of the similarity in symptoms. When you get correctly diagnosed for BPD, you start to research it also and read the experiences of other people as the understanding of why your life is the way it is suddenly beginning to fall into place. Every information you come across seems to describe you perfectly.

For the first time you realize you are not alone, there are others just like you, it begins the first big step in getting more in control over the condition. You cry, you laugh and tell yourself you can do it. As you learn more and more about you, you realize there are many overlaps of BPD symptoms with other mental health challenges like anxiety and depression. You have to deal with those other symptoms usually make the effect of the BPD on you more intense on several occasions, yet sometimes you can manage the situation better.

You finally begin understanding why you sometimes wanted to resort to self-harm and why suicide always seems like the best option. You learn that the statistics BPD who attempt suicide at some point is about 70 percent and recognize you make up part of that number. Fortunately, however, you are so far fortunate not to be part of the one out of every ten that are successful in their suicide attempt. Absorbing all this information can get daunting.

Chapter 10
Life after the Diagnosis

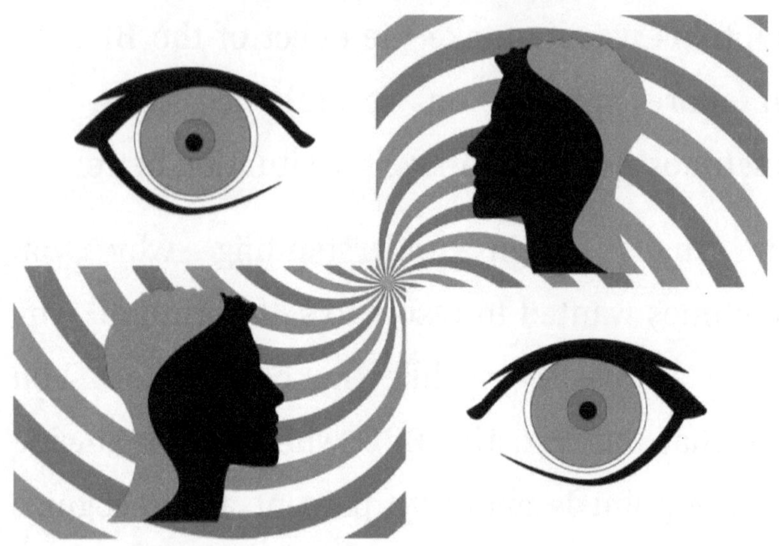

Diagnosis also comes with consequences, and you find that you now have difficulty knowing when to trust your brain's interpretation of a situation and how you should respond to it appropriately. You are no longer certain if it is you been paranoia of what somebody else did was as hurtful as you have interpreted it to be. Next, there is the other flip of not correctly recognizing a really bad situation for what it is because you are trying to compensate for your BPD.

You also get to realize that being diagnosed is one thing, getting help is another thing. First, professional help is expensive, secondly, there are not many insurance schemes that cover the BPD type of mental health. And if you are on Medicaid, it can be worse because you could have a hard time trying to get a doctor that was qualified enough to handle your case and in the rare case that you found one, your time on the waiting list could be up to 6 months.

Getting professional help will probably be one of the best decisions you would have made in life. You learn from your various research that the journey is a long one, you now know your diagnosis is only the first step in the long journey ahead, yet nothing seems to prepare you for the difficult moments ahead. By now you have had the process of therapy started and have started attending various sections and put on a treatment plan where you are instantly told that the success or failure of that plan depends on you.

Sometimes you go through with the process and make considerable progress, sometimes you suffer a relapse and end up in hospital units that also deal with pre and postpartum related issues. You find you are beginning to balance out and ready to be receptive again to therapy and ready to go, even then you see the look of concern and disbelief from loved ones, and the professionals who seem to have heard that in all their careers and treat it with a pinch of salt.

Sometimes you are informed you could come multiple times in a week and be a part of both group and individual sessions. You are also encouraged to read self-help books, listen to motivational recordings and undertake some self-guided activities in the long journey towards living a normal life. You find out that the whole process can be super hard. Mental health care in the U.S. can be plain ridiculous.

Then there is the issue of not believing your own emotions. You are no longer able to distinguish between the real aspects of your feelings from when you are just overreacting. You become constantly at war with yourself if you are justified over situations you are agitated about. This situation can leave you vulnerable and set the stage for people to take advantage of you and subject you to abusive behaviors, because the imbalance in your emotions which you are trying to control can cause you to try and justify the things people do for you by believing you are simply overreacting when in the real sense, you are the victim in this case. Having someone who understands and loves you well enough to put in the amount of sacrifice towards helping through the journey can help to ease the process.

Handling Relationships Better

You are now learning from therapeutic sessions how some of your actions may have affected your relationships negatively and you are determined to make the next one a success. One possible advice you will get will be to be very open to your prospective partners about who you are and what to expect if they are to follow through with being in a relationship with you. If you inform them very early that there will be moments when your words and actions will be such that seem to suggest you are trying to push them away, they should understand that you in fact desperately want them to hold you in. It may sound crazy at first, but it is what it is. You should make them realize you are not trying to push them away, and if they are ready to put up with it, then you are going to make an effort on your part to put up a fight to reduce the number of times you resort to hurtful words and emotional outburst. If the person is serious enough about the relationship, they will make an effort and be proactive in their own to research on a BPD condition to the extent that they will become supportive and sometimes in a way no member of your family ever was. You will be pleasantly surprised that they can be so active in their support by helping to search out groups, doctors, and therapists that can help with the management of your therapeutic process. On days when you have your dreadful moments and go out in intense rage and outbursts, they will be better equipped to recognize it and more informed on how best to deal with it. They will be many such moments, but with the self-awareness from both of you, you are better capable to deal with it and recognize what you had just done as really bad and awful, which can encourage you to work better and sustain your relationship.

Getting Help and Therapy

Therapy for BPD will almost always consist of Dialectical Behavioral Therapy (DBT), which is a form of CBT designed specially to be used in the treatment of borderline. This form of treatment is designed to better help you in managing your life and your symptoms more effectively. BPD is more or less something you will have to experience for the rest of your life, although you will likely learn that there are no medications for BPD and that it tends to ease off as you get older. You will probably notice you tend to manage better on the days you take your medication than on the days that you do not.

Even though BPD itself does not have a medication for treating it, at least as at the time this book was written, in your experience, you will probably notice that many mental health professionals will tend to give you antidepressants and anti-anxiety medications to help you treat other sideline mental health issues like anxiety, stress, and depression that go along with BPD. As for the BPD itself, the only real way you will be told to manage it will be with DBT, which tends to focus a lot on emotional regulation, mindfulness, how to avoid triggers, self-harm, and unhealthy behaviors. The whole essence of DBT is to retrain your brain so that self-harm, rage, substance abuse and all the other negative symptoms are not the first things you consider in your moment of crisis. You will also find it is a learning process that does take time.

Another thing that may also shock you will be that you will be turned back by some therapist as soon as they recognize that you are a BPD. You cannot blame them though, in the cycle of many mental health professionals, BPD is considered one of the most difficult mental health issues to handle which is why many will prefer to have nothing to do with it. Some will tell you that they are not qualified to handle a case of such magnitude, preferring instead to refer you to some more qualified persons.

In most DBT centers, where BPD is part of their specialty, your treatment plan will typically include individual sessions and group sessions at different days of the week. Many times, they are not cheap and if you do not manage your finances properly, it can put you in debt or many other things in the family, especially the kids' welfare can take the heat.

Your Concerns about your Kids

One fear you will have at the back of your mind as a BPD will be the issue of if the condition is a hereditary one or not and wish not to have any of your kids experience a life that you have gone through. You know it is hard enough for them just being around you, wondering if you are equipped enough to cater for them, but for you will not wish the condition for even your enemy much less your kids.

Scientists are still not sure where BPD comes from, but the general belief is that BPD is a combination of genes and the environment. It is believed that if a child is exposed to some amount of emotional trauma in childhood, it can trigger a disorder in their personality including BPD. If you are a responsible parent, you will always have that huge fear that you could be passing it off to your kids.

BPD is an ailment that seems not to be able to hide so that even with your best effort and against your will, you could find you hurt the people that you care about the most. Yet out of the people you want to hurt, you will be desperate for your kids not to be one of them. You recognize they are innocent victims that deserve better and should not be made to go through a life where they are constantly subjected to such emotional abuse and psychological trauma.

The memory of your early experiences and how difficult it was to reach out to those around is still fresh in your brain. You want to try and use your own experience and the extra knowledge you have acquired along the way to be a more sympathetic ear and be able to provide a sort of first-line intervention if you do pass any of the symptoms to them. You would wish to be able to help them better and ease their suffering even though you would rather they did not have it at all.

Ultimately, you will recognize that you can only handle how you can interact with them and not what struggles they eventually end up dealing with in life. You will only wish to arm yourself with better coping skills and ways to be proactive when dealing with them.

Many a time, even if you do not feel like going for your weekly sessions, the thoughts of the kind of life you want to give to your kids serve as an extra motivation to continue your therapy in an attempt to get better and be the best parent and partner you can be.

To Sum it Up

Each Day is a Constant Struggle

You will find that a life with BPD is difficult to explain, with each day a constant war between the forces that require you to accept what your brain wants you to implement in certain situations and forces that want you to adopt the more rational approach that a person who does not have BPD will take in their reaction to similar issues.

You wish others were less judgmental of you and do not see you as a monster or someone who intentionally wants to manipulate those around them. You wish they understood that you do not desire to be mean or to hurt anyone, that they see you as a victim of a far more superior force bigger than you can handle with the limited skills you have. You also wish they were more appreciative of the little efforts you are putting to aspire to be better, healthier and sane. To do this, you have to fight with every fiber of your body when trying to resist the forces against you acting normal. Sometimes you cry, you fight, you shout, you even go to the extent of hurting yourself as a way of dealing with your personal struggles being the only way you know how to deal with the situation.

Every Emotion is Either Full or Empty

The duplicity of the emotions of a borderline personality is what puzzles a lot of people. One moment you are a lovely company to be with and you so idolized the people around you, then the next moment you are in a fit of rage over what others would have overlooked completely. You are either completely depressed when depressed and very happy when you are happy. In moments when you consider the people in your life as bad, you completely shut them off, and later you accuse them of abandoning you.

You will also observe that you are not always able to recognize the things that get you depressed, but you know that the feeling is not pleasant because it leaves you broken with no reason to go on. The feeling can be so severe that it would seem like sinking into the deepest pit imaginable and leave you hanging on just your previous experience of knowing it would pass like others before it.

However, your experience on the flip side is such an intense one; the joy, happiness, love, all cumulate into an experience that you wish will never come to an end.

In relationships, you are sometimes wholly committed to the person, adoring and imagining the person to be the next best thing to have happened to you, yet not too long after you find that you are so scared of committing to anyone and completely lose your affection for the person and leave them. You can feel absolutely nothing for them at one moment, and the next moment is filled with more than 20 emotions at once, leaving you physically and emotionally drained.

Therefore, a friend of many years can become bad in your mind, especially if they inadvertently do something you perceive as bad even if it is something as trivial as putting the wrong quantity of sugar in your tea. A whole experience of a vacation can also be ruined if the waiter created a negative impression in your mind during your outing. If your boyfriend makes a comment about your outfit in a non-complimentary way, you can instantly start wanting to call off the relationship and assume you would enjoy a better life being single, yet when he makes you tea while you are still on the bed, he becomes the best man in the world.

Trust is a Luxury You Cannot Afford

Your life as a BPD is going to be frequently characterized by a lack of trust where you believe everyone around you is out to deliberately hurt you. The feeling that no one can be trusted because you tend to over-analyze all their actions while searching for reasons to justify why you feel they do not care about you. Whatever hurt you feel is internalized because you assume that it is something you deserve and then when the occasion arises, you unleash the hurt on the people you hold dear.

Your Default Reaction is to Constantly Assume the Worst

As a BPD person, you will consistently have to deal with your default negative emotions. Not many people can understand how highly active your brain becomes and over-analyzed situations with the resultant outcome being only the most pessimistic scenario. You imagine that your kids are going to get hit by a drunk driver if they were on their way to school, sometimes become paranoid about it to the extent that you imagine you presumably have to get pregnant and give birth to another child to replace the child that will die or possibly consider adopting a child instead.

Or, it could be that you imagine that your husband is going to suffer a work-related accident that will affect the finances of the family and you start developing some sort of animosity towards him for abandoning the family in death. You know deep down that these thoughts are irrational and a symptom of your disorder.

You Feel Like You are Just a Passenger in your Body

You imagine yourself to be a passenger residing inside your body and with someone else in the driver's seat. You are completely removed and dissociated from reality. Therefore, while you can harbor intense feelings about situations, you are equally able to go numb, detached and reactionless to similar situations. You seem to have no form of control over the things you feel as you do bizarre things, hoping to keep people to stay with you when in fact your actions drive them away. As a result, you have difficulties developing any meaningful relationship or maintaining any connection with people.

You Desire Validation as If Your Life Depended on It

Your life is usually one that seems to be broken when in all probability you genuinely do not quite understand yourself, yet you employ a greater part of your life wishing you were better understood, accepted, and validated. Your diagnosis as a BPD seems to provide the excellent cover to seek for validation and an excuse to act in irrational ways as you burn all your bridges, end your relationship, cheat, steal and even ignore psychotherapy that is designed to encourage you to address the very problems you are having. No one understands what it feels like to be unable to manage the flow of your emotions, understand boundaries and how ill-equipped you are to live a better life for yourself.

Everything seems Absurd and Crazy

As a BPD, you are likely to consistently experience an internal conflict that makes you convinced that you are alone in the middle of a crazy world. You wonder how else it is to describe a person who is incapable of holding a steady job even jobs that others would kill for. You wonder if the feeling of being lonely yet not able to interact with other people is not being insane. It can get confusing when you possess this personality. You sometimes wish you could get other people to feel what you feel for one day and go through the riotous emotions that you feel for a couple of hours so that they know what it is like someone who wants to be alone and still miss the presence of people, how you try to separate the warring parties in your head who seem determined to fight another world war inside the small space. In all of these situations, you realize you need help, but you are unwilling to subject yourself to professional help because you do not believe in them.

You know you are Different

With the amount of hurt, you constantly feel, you cannot help but feel different, always wishing your life could be a happy one like that of those around you instead of the hurting one you constantly feel inside. Your emotions, as a BPD is a magnified form of the type of emotions that others feel, which probably explains why there are no gray areas for you. So, your life is consistently about trying to get reassurance that the other person is not mad at you or the number of times your feelings get hurt in a never-ending cycle even though you know it is not normal. You constantly seem to have some special chemicals in your brain that make you annoy the people in your life because of your emotional pain, which then causes you to desire complete isolation even though you are aching in your bones for the people around you to stay.